TOP TENS

FIERCE PREDATORS

1 GREAT WHITE SHARK

2 ORCA (KILLER WHALE)

3 AFRICAN LION

4 NILE CROCODILE

5 GREAT HORNED OWL

6 CHEETAH

7 ROYAL BENGAL TIGER

8 POLAR BEAR

9 COYOTE

10 LEOPARD

Copyright ' ticktock Entertainment Ltd 2006
First published in Great Britain in 2005 by ticktock Media Ltd,
Unit 2, Orchard Business Centre, North Farm Road, Tunbridge Wells, Kent TN2 3XF
ISBN 978 1 86007 912 2 pbk
Printed in China
9 8 7 6 5 4 3 2
A CIP catalogue record for this book is available from the British Library.

Picture credits (t=top; b=bottom; c=centre; l=left; r=right): Corbis: 6-7 all, 9t, 10-11 all, 12-13 all, 14-15 all, 16-17 all, 20-21 all, 26t. FLPA: 8-9c, 18-19 all, 22-23 all, 24-25 all, 27 all.

Every effort has been made to trace the copyright holders, and we apologise in advance for any unintentional omissions. We would be pleased to insert the appropriate acknowledgements in any subsequent edition of this publication.

CONTENTS

This book is a catalogue of the world's top ten predators. Predators are nature's born killers, it is what they do - they must kill in order to eat. There are many different animals that are predators, including mammals, birds, reptiles and fish. But which is the best? Our top ten predators were rated according to:

BODY MASS

Size is obviously important for a predator. The bigger the predator, the bigger the prey it can attack. Similarly with weight, a heavy predator will find it easier to drag down and overpower its prey. We gave our predators a combined score based on their size and weight, but also taking into consideration the average size of their prey in each case.

NO.1 GREAT WHITE SHARK

The great white shark is the world's deadliest and most dangerous **predator**. It is found near cool and **temperate** coastlines across the globe. Armed with jaws more than 60 centimetres wide, the great white shark has a superb sense of smell and can detect wounded **prey** several miles away.

BODY MASS
Measuring up to 8 metres in length, a great white shark can weigh more than 3,000 kilograms.

SPEED
It is a fast swimmer, especially when chasing prey, and can leap its entire body out of the water.

TEETH AND CLAWS
Rows of triangular teeth line the great white's massive jaws. Each tooth is **serrated** like a steak knife and is razor sharp.

KILLER INSTINCT
The great white attacks prey with a twisting lunge tearing a chunk of flesh from the victim. The shark then retreats and waits for the victim to die from loss of blood.

24

SPEED

High speed gives a predator a tremendous advantage. The cheetah, which is the world's fastest animal, was clearly the winner in this category. With the others, we also looked at whether the animals could leap, and how far. We also gave extra points to crocodiles because they can move on land as well as in water.

TEETH AND CLAWS

This category examines the tools of the predators' trade – the deadly weapons that are used to kill their prey.

We based our score on the number, length and sharpness of the teeth and claws of each predator. These scores were adjusted according to whether it is the teeth or the claws that are the primary offensive weapons.

KILLER INSTINCT

Here we look at the overall style of each predator's attack. We gave points for hunting technique, stealth and camouflage. Additional points went to those predators that were able to achieve the all-important element of surprise, taking their prey unawares. We also gave bonus points to those animals that had highly developed senses for locating prey.

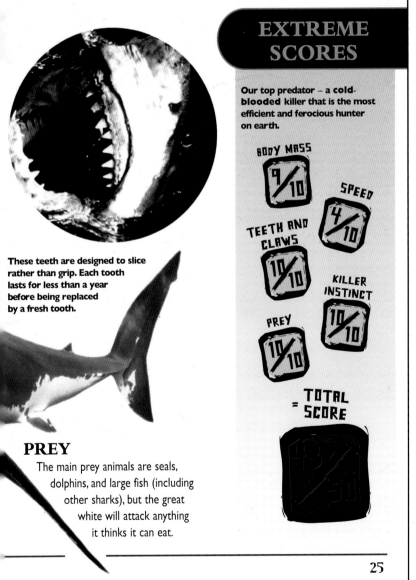

These teeth are designed to slice rather than grip. Each tooth lasts for less than a year before being replaced by a fresh tooth.

PREY

The main prey animals are seals, dolphins, and large fish (including other sharks), but the great white will attack anything it thinks it can eat.

EXTREME SCORES

Our top predator – a cold-blooded killer that is the most efficient and ferocious hunter on earth.

BODY MASS
9/10

SPEED
4/10

TEETH AND CLAWS
10/10

KILLER INSTINCT
10/10

PREY
10/10

= TOTAL SCORE

PREY

Few predators specialize in just one kind of prey. Most are generalists that will attack anything that they can kill and eat – especially if they have not eaten for some time and are very hungry. Points were allocated according to the size and variety of prey that is normally taken. Extra points went to those predators that sometimes feast on human flesh.

The leopard is a secretive and deadly **predator** that only comes out to hunt at night. Powerful limb and neck muscles make it the strongest climber of the big cats.
The leopard lives in warm and cool climates throughout Asia and Africa, and is found in both open country and dense forest.

BODY MASS

This agile hunter weighs about 65 kilograms. Most leopards have pale fur with black spots, but some are entirely black. These black leopards are known as panthers.

SPEED

Very few people have ever seen a leopard run at top speed, but it can reach about 37 mph and can leap across a gap 6 metres wide.

TEETH AND CLAWS

The leopard has broad paws with curved claws that end in very sharp points. Its canine teeth are longer proportionally than in any other big cat.

Spotted fur provides excellent camouflage when stalking prey.

KILLER INSTINCT

This big cat may sneak up on its **prey** through tall grass. Or it may wait in ambush on a tree branch, before jumping down to sink its teeth into its victim's neck.

PREY

Although it can attack and kill prey as big as a giraffe, the leopard mainly hunts smaller **mammals** such as **antelope**, deer and wild pigs.

Eyes positioned at the front of the head indicate that this animal is a predator.

This **nocturnal predator** is a deadly killer that combines stealth with powerful muscles and sharp claws.

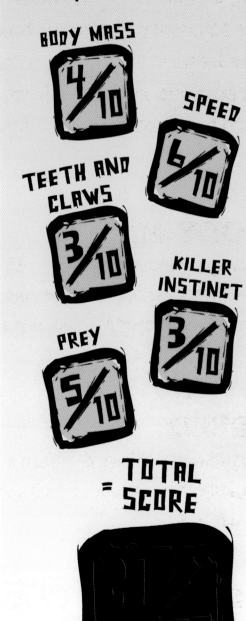

BODY MASS
4/10

SPEED
6/10

TEETH AND CLAWS
3/10

KILLER INSTINCT
3/10

PREY
5/10

= TOTAL SCORE

COYOTE

The coyote is a North American wild dog that has adapted to a wide variety of environments. It is found from the hot deserts of Mexico to the frozen forests of Alaska and northern Canada. The coyote is a highly efficient **predator** that hunts by both night and day.

BODY MASS

The coyote is about the size of a German shepherd dog, but much slimmer. The average coyote weighs about 14 kg, and the male is slightly heavier than the female.

SPEED

Coyotes can run at speeds of up to 30 mph for short burst but can maintain a 20 mph lope for long periods.

TEETH AND CLAWS

Its claws are sharp, but teeth are the coyote's main weapons. There are 42 in all, including four long, pointed canine teeth.

A coyote uses its eyes, ears and nose to locate its prey.

Parents fetch food for young coyote pups.

KILLER INSTINCT

The coyote usually hunts alone, and can chase **prey** over long distances without getting tired. It has an excellent sense of smell for sniffing out prey hiding underground.

PREY

The coyote hunts a wide variety of prey; mainly small **mammals**, such as mice, rabbits and squirrels, but also birds, snakes, and lizards. It will also kill cats and dogs in urban areas.

Snow, rock, grassland or desert – it's all the same to this **adaptable** predator.

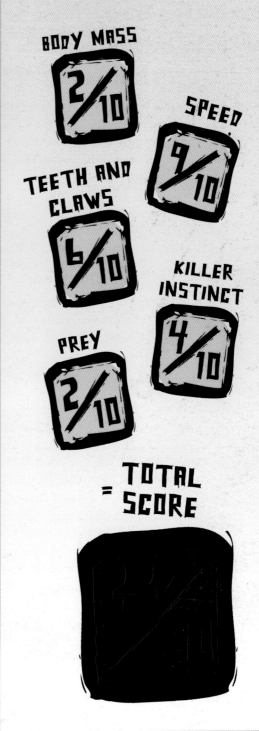

BODY MASS
2/10

SPEED
9/10

TEETH AND CLAWS
6/10

KILLER INSTINCT
4/10

PREY
2/10

= TOTAL SCORE

The polar bear lives in the Arctic region surrounding the North Pole. It is the largest and most powerful predator that lives on land, and it has nothing to fear – except hunger. A polar bear needs to spend about half its waking life hunting, because it is only successful one or two times in every hundred attempts.

BODY MASS

A polar bear has a huge body covered in shaggy fur. It can weigh up to 700 kilograms and is more than 3 metres long.

TEETH AND CLAWS

It has long, sharp claws that can easily rip through skin and muscle. Its powerful **jaws** can crunch through bones.

PREY

The main food items are seals, but polar bears also **prey** on fish, seabirds, walruses and reindeer.

Pale fur provides camouflage against the snow-covered landscape.

Powerful muscles are the key to the polar bear's deadly attack.

Insulated from the cold by a thick fur coat, this Arctic killer is a powerful predator.

KILLER INSTINCT

The polar bear usually catches seals when they are out of the water or come to the surface to breathe. Sometimes a polar bear will break through ice to get at a seal underneath.

SPEED

A polar bear can run across snow and ice at speeds of up to 25 mph. It is also an excellent swimmer.

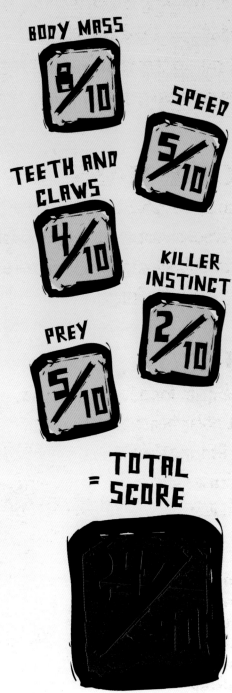

BODY MASS
8/10

SPEED
5/10

TEETH AND CLAWS
4/10

KILLER INSTINCT
2/10

PREY
5/10

= TOTAL SCORE

11

ROYAL BENGAL TIGER

The Royal Bengal tiger is one of the largest of the tiger sub-species, and it rivals the Siberian tiger for the title "Biggest of the Big Cats". The Royal Bengal tiger is found in parts of northern India and Pakistan. Like all tigers, it is a deadly predator, and it can develop a taste for human flesh.

BODY MASS

The Royal Bengal tiger is the second-largest tiger in the world. It weighs between 200-250 kilograms, and can measure 2.8 metres in length.

No two tigers have exactly the same pattern of stripes.

SPEED

This tiger is one of the fastest animals in the world. They can only sprint for a short distance, but these tigers can reach speeds of nearly 38 mph.

This predator leaps onto its prey with claws outstretched and jaw gaping wide.

TEETH AND CLAWS

The Royal Bengal tiger has strong, sharp claws and powerful **jaws** equipped with 30 sharp teeth. It has the biggest canine teeth of any animal in the world.

KILLER INSTINCT

Royal Bengal tigers leap onto their prey, digging in with their claws to drag their victim to the ground.

PREY

This tiger will attack animals larger than itself, and its main prey is deer. It can eat more than 40 kilograms of meat at a time.

The tiger is the largest and most awesome of the big cats. It is a born predator.

BODY MASS
6/10

SPEED
7/10

TEETH AND CLAWS
4/10

KILLER INSTINCT
5/10

PREY
3/10

= TOTAL SCORE

CHEETAH

The cheetah is the fastest thing on four legs – it can run quicker than any other animal on Earth. The superfast cheetah is one of the smallest of the big cats, but it is also one of the deadliest. The cheetah lives on the grasslands of Africa, where it uses its speed to catch fast-running prey.

BODY MASS

The cheetah has a slim, lightweight body, and weighs only about 40-45 kilograms.

The cheetah has a very distinctive body shape.

SPEED

Over short distances a cheetah can reach a speed of nearly 70 mph.

TEETH AND CLAWS

The cheetah attacks with both teeth and claws in a highly efficient "catch and cling" technique.

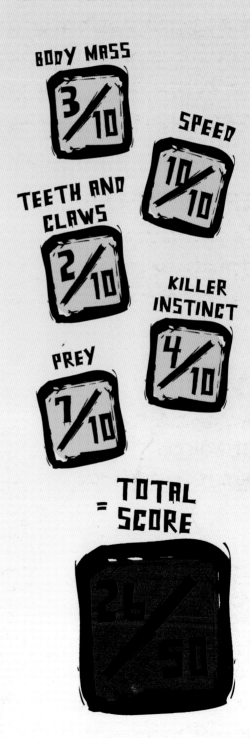

Sharp claws and teeth drag down
a helpless victim.

KILLER INSTINCT

A cheetah usually hunts during sunrise
and sunset. It will stealthily creep
through the grass until it is
close enough to its prey to
launch a high-speed attack.

PREY

The cheetah hunts
rabbits and small
mammals, as well as
larger prey such as
zebra and **antelope**.

No animal can run fast enough
to escape the high-speed attack
launched by this predator.

BODY MASS
3/10

SPEED
10/10

TEETH AND CLAWS
2/10

KILLER INSTINCT
4/10

PREY
7/10

= TOTAL SCORE
25/50

GREAT HORNED OWL

The great horned owl is a deadly **predator** that can kill **prey** up to three times its own size. It is so deadly that it has earned the nickname "the tiger of the woods". The great horned owl is found throughout North, Central and South America and lives in abandoned nests, trees or even caves.

BODY MASS

The great horned owl weighs about 2.5 kilograms and stands over half a metre tall with a wingspan of up to a metre and a half. Females are larger than males.

SPEED

This majestic bird has a maximum flying speed of nearly 38 mph. It attacks silently and without warning, swooping down from its perch to seize its prey on the ground.

TEETH AND CLAWS

The great horned owl has no teeth, but it does have a sharp **beak** for tearing flesh. Its main weapons are the sharp pointed **talons** on its feet.

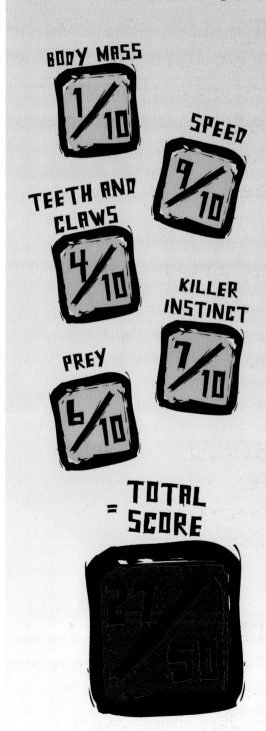

Sharp eyes and keen hearing are the key to the owl's success as a hunter.

KILLER INSTINCT

The great horned owl is most active at night. They use their sense of sight and hearing to find prey. They are stealth hunters and dive down from high perches to snatch their prey.

PREY

A great horned owl is capable of taking prey much bigger than itself. Its diet includes skunks, foxes and even porcupines.

The colouration of the feathers provides excellent **camouflage** against tree trunks and branches.

This bird is a silent killer that swoops down out of the darkness without warning.

BODY MASS
1/10

SPEED
9/10

TEETH AND CLAWS
4/10

KILLER INSTINCT
7/10

PREY
6/10

= TOTAL SCORE
27/50

The Nile crocodile is found in rivers, lakes and swamps throughout most of Africa. It is a **cold-blooded** killer, but rather a lazy hunter. This large **reptile** prefers to lie in ambush, with only its eyes and **nostrils** showing above the river surface, waiting for **prey** to come near enough for it to strike.

BODY MASS

Nile crocodiles can grow up to 6 metres in length. They are covered in natural armour made of bony plates embedded in the skin.

A crocodile swims by using its flattened tail as a paddle.

TEETH AND CLAWS

The claws are fairly blunt and are mainly used for digging nests in the riverbank. Long **jaws** full of sharp teeth are the Nile crocodile's main weapons.

SPEED

The Nile crocodile swims at about 4-6 mph. On land it can run at almost twice that speed.

These long, sharp teeth can inflict terrible wounds.

KILLER INSTINCT

Like other reptiles, the Nile crocodile can bite, but it cannot chew. Small prey is swallowed whole. Larger prey is grabbed and dragged underwater to drown.

PREY

Small prey includes fish and water birds, but animals as big as buffalos and giraffe are attacked when they drink or wade across rivers.

At first glance it might look like a log of wood floating in the water – but that "log" is actually one of the most feared of all predators.

BODY MASS
7/10

SPEED
3/10

TEETH AND CLAWS
8/10

KILLER INSTINCT
8/10

PREY
6/10

= TOTAL SCORE
32/50

Although it is famous as the "King of the Jungle", the African lion is rarely seen in a rain forest environment. This powerful **predator** prefers the open grasslands of the savannah or veldt. Unlike other big cats, which are usually solitary hunters, the African lion often hunts in small groups of between three and eight animals.

BODY MASS

African lions can reach lengths of over 3 metres, and can weigh up to 250 kilograms. The male is larger than the female lioness.

SPEED

The African lion is not a good or fast runner, but it can reach about 34 mph over very short distances.

TEETH AND CLAWS

These lions have five claws on each paw. Its powerful **jaws** are packed full with 30 sharp teeth that can lock together like a vice.

The lion is Africa's top predator.

Male lions are the only big cats with a mane of long fur.

KILLER INSTINCT

Lions usually co-operate with each other when hunting. Several members of a lion group will try to drive the prey towards other lions.

PREY

The African lion hunts mainly large **mammals**. These **prey** include zebra, gnus, impala and wildebeest.

The technique of cooperative hunting gives this big cat a deadly advantage over all the others.

BODY MASS
6/10

SPEED
8/10

TEETH AND CLAWS
5/10

KILLER INSTINCT
7/10

PREY
8/10

= TOTAL SCORE

The orca, or killer whale, is a toothed whale that is closely related to dolphins and porpoises. This marine mammal is found in seas and oceans around the world, although it prefers cooler water and is rarely seen in the tropics. The orca deserves its popular name because it is a deadly, top predator with no natural enemies.

BODY MASS

A fully-grown orca normally measures around 7 metres but lengths of nearly 10 metres have been recorded! These whales can weigh up to 10,000 kilograms. Males are bigger than the females.

The orca has a distinctive black-and-white colouration.

SPEED

Orcas are fast swimmers. They can reach over 30 mph in short bursts when chasing their prey.

TEETH AND CLAWS

An orca has 40-46 large, pointed teeth, but it cannot chew and has to swallow its prey whole.

KILLER INSTINCT

Orcas often live and hunt in small family groups that are known as pods, and the members of a pod often co-operate while hunting. Individual orcas will even seize sea lions that are resting on a beach.

The smiling face of a born killer.

This is one of the biggest predators on Earth – about 10 tonnes of killing power.

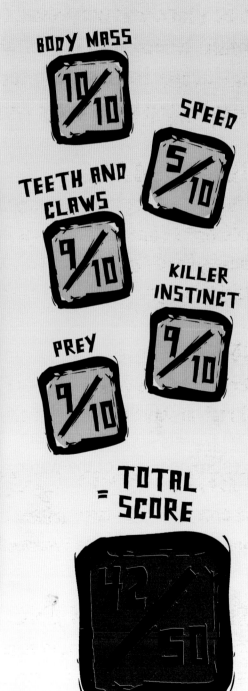

BODY MASS
10/10

SPEED
5/10

TEETH AND CLAWS
9/10

KILLER INSTINCT
9/10

PREY
9/10

= TOTAL SCORE

42/50

PREY

The orca feeds mainly on fish (especially salmon), but it also hunts dolphins, whales, squid, seals, sea lions, penguins, and marine turtles.

The great white shark is the world's deadliest and most dangerous **predator**. It is found near cool and **temperate** coastlines across the globe. Armed with jaws more than 60 centimetres wide, the great white shark has a superb sense of smell and can detect wounded **prey** several miles away.

BODY MASS

Measuring up to 8 metres in length, a great white shark can weigh more than 3,000 kilograms.

SPEED

It is a fast swimmer, especially when chasing prey, and can leap its entire body out of the water.

TEETH AND CLAWS

Rows of triangular teeth line the great white's massive jaws. Each tooth is **serrated** like a steak knife and is razor sharp.

KILLER INSTINCT

The great white attacks prey with a twisting lunge tearing a chunk of flesh from the victim. The shark then retreats and waits for the victim to die from loss of blood.

These teeth are designed to slice rather than grip. Each tooth lasts for less than a year before being replaced by a fresh tooth.

PREY

The main prey animals are seals, dolphins, and large fish (including other sharks), but the great white will attack anything it thinks it can eat.

Our top predator – a **cold-blooded** killer that is the most efficient and ferocious hunter on earth.

BODY MASS
9/10

SPEED
4/10

TEETH AND CLAWS
10/10

KILLER INSTINCT
10/10

PREY
10/10

= TOTAL SCORE

Before deciding our Top Ten Predators, we also considered these animals – all of them are skilled and efficient hunters, but they are not quite good enough to make the Top Ten.

BALD EAGLE

The bald eagle is the national bird of the United States of America. It is not really bald, but the white feathers on its head and neck make it look bald from a distance. It is a large, powerful bird that weighs up to 6 kilograms and has a wingspan of up to 2.5 metres. The bald eagle is especially fond of fish, and swoops down to seize salmon in its sharp **talons**.

TARANTULA

Tarantulas are the largest of all spiders and they are widespread throughout **tropical** regions. The biggest tarantulas have a leg span of nearly 30 centimetres and can move very quickly. Tarantulas do not spin webs; they are active hunters that prowl around at night looking for **prey** such as mice and small birds.

VAMPIRE BAT

This small South American **mammal** has a fearsome reputation because of its diet — it feeds on the blood of other mammals. The vampire bat does not actually suck blood; it bites its victim to make the blood flow, then laps it up with its tongue. Although it can fly, this bat likes to walk and it is more likely to attack its prey from the ground.

WOLVERINE

The wolverine is the largest and fiercest member of the weasel family. It lives in the coniferous forests of Europe, Asia and North America. The wolverine measures up to 1.5 metres from nose to tail, and weighs about 15 kilograms. It chases after small prey such as hares and rabbits; and will climb trees so that it can jump down on large prey such as deer.

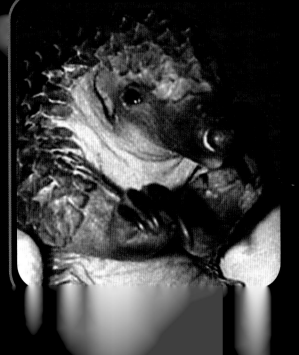

PANGOLIN

This strange scale-covered mammal is found in Africa and Asia. Although it is not at all fierce, the pangolin is in its own way a mighty hunter. It uses its powerful claws to burrow into termite mounds and ant nests, and then slurps up their tasty eggs with its long tongue. The unique coat of hard scales protects the pangolin against ant bites and stings.

NO. 10 LEOPARD

Scientific name	*Panthera pardus*	**Extreme Scores**	
Animal type	*Mammal*	**Body mass**	4
Location	*Africa, Asia*	**Speed**	6
Size	*2 m*	**Teeth & Claws**	3
Habitat	*Grasslands and forest*	**Killer instinct**	3
Notable Feature	*Agility*	**Prey**	5

TOTAL SCORE 21 / 50

NO. 9 COYOTE

Scientific name	*Canis latrans*	**Extreme Scores**	
Animal type	*Mammal*	**Body mass**	2
Location	*North and Central America*	**Speed**	9
Size	*95 cm*	**Teeth & Claws**	6
Habitat	*Deserts, mountains, praries*	**Killer instinct**	4
Notable Feature	*Hardy, sense of smell*	**Prey**	2

TOTAL SCORE 23 / 50

NO. 8 POLAR BEAR

Scientific name	*Ursus maritimus*	**Extreme Scores**	
Animal type	*Mammal*	**Body mass**	8
Location	*Artic*	**Speed**	5
Size	*3.4 m*	**Teeth & Claws**	4
Habitat	*Arctic region*	**Killer instinct**	2
Notable Feature	*Bulk and power*	**Prey**	5

TOTAL SCORE 24 / 50

NO. 7 ROYAL BENGAL TIGER

Scientific name	*Panther tigris tigris*	**Extreme Scores**	
Animal type	*Mammal*	**Body mass**	6
Location	*Asia*	**Speed**	7
Size	*2.8 m*	**Teeth & Claws**	4
Habitat	*Forests, jungles and swamps*	**Killer instinct**	5
Notable Feature	*Large canine teeth*	**Prey**	3

TOTAL SCORE 24 / 50

NO. 6 CHEETAH

Scientific name	*Acinonyx jubatus*	**Extreme Scores**	
Animal type	*Mammal*	**Body mass**	3
Location	*Africa*	**Speed**	10
Size	*1.5 m*	**Teeth & Claws**	2
Habitat	*Grasslands*	**Killer instinct**	4
Notable Feature	*Speed*	**Prey**	7

TOTAL SCORE 26 / 50

NO. 5 GREAT HORNED OWL

		Extreme Scores	
Scientific name	*Bubo virginianus*		
Animal type	Bird	Body mass	1
Location	The Americas	Speed	9
Size	60 cm	Teeth & Claws	4
Habitat	Forest, woodland, shrubland	Killer instinct	7
Notable Feature	Keen sight	Prey	6

TOTAL SCORE 27 / 50

NO. 4 NILE CROCODILE

		Extreme Scores	
Scientific name	*Crocodylus niloticus*		
Animal type	Reptile	Body mass	7
Location	Africa	Speed	3
Size	6 m	Teeth & Claws	8
Habitat	Rivers, lakes, marshes	Killer instinct	8
Notable Feature	Powerful jaws	Prey	6

TOTAL SCORE 32 / 50

NO. 3 AFRICAN LION

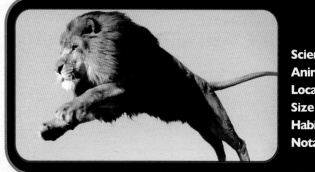

		Extreme Scores	
Scientific name	*Panthera leo*		
Animal type	Mammal	Body mass	6
Location	Africa	Speed	8
Size	2.5 m	Teeth & Claws	5
Habitat	Savannah	Killer instinct	7
Notable Feature	Strength	Prey	8

TOTAL SCORE 34 / 50

NO. 2 ORCA (KILLER WHALE)

		Extreme Scores	
Scientific name	*Orcinus orca*		
Animal type	Mammal	Body mass	10
Location	Worldwide	Speed	5
Size	7 m	Teeth & Claws	9
Habitat	Seas and oceans	Killer instinct	9
Notable Feature	Size and speed	Prey	9

TOTAL SCORE 42 / 50

NO. 1 GREAT WHITE SHARK

		Extreme Scores	
Scientific name	*Carcharodon carcharias*		
Animal type	Cartilaginous fish	Body mass	9
Location	Worldwide	Speed	4
Size	8 m	Teeth & Claws	10
Habitat	Coastal and offshore waters	Killer instinct	10
Notable Feature	Killer instinct	Prey	10

TOTAL SCORE 43 / 50

ADAPTABLE capable of adapting to a particular situation or use

ANTELOPE group of fast-running, grass-eating mammals native to Africa and Asia, with long horns and a slender build

ARCTIC regions around the North Pole

BEAK a bird's jaws

CAMOUFLAGE the natural colour or markings of an animal that enable it to blend in with its surroundings

CARNIVORE a meat-eating animal

COLD-BLOODED an animal whose body temperature is not internally regulated

JAWS structures that form the framework of the mouth and hold the teeth

MAMMAL any of various warm-blooded animals with a covering of hair on the skin and, in the female, the ability to produce milk with which to feed the young.

MARINE something of, relating to, or produced by the sea

NOCTURNAL a creature that is active during the night

NOSTRILS either of the external openings of the nose

PREDATOR an animal that lives by preying on other animals

PREY an animal hunted or caught for food

REPTILE a cold-blooded animal that has scales and lays eggs on land

SAVANNAH flat grassland of tropical or subtropical regions

SERRATED notched like the edge of a saw

SUB-SPECIES subdivision (a race or variety) of a species

TALON the claw of a bird of prey or predatory animal

TEMPERATE a region free from extremes of temperature

TROPICAL hot and humid; relating to the tropics, a region on either side of the equator

VELDT open grazing areas of southern Africa